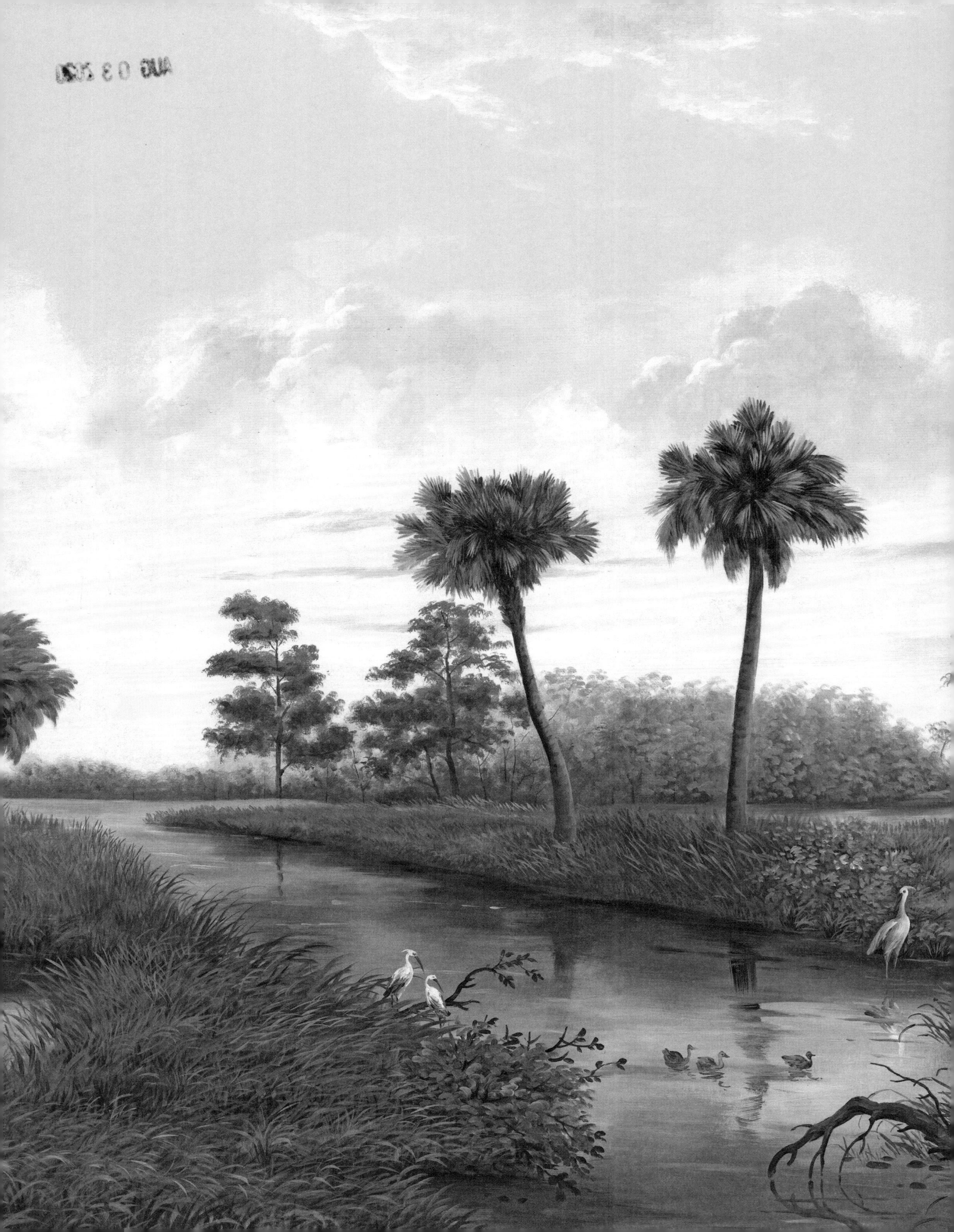

ARRIVING HOME

ARRIVING HOME

A Gracious Southern Welcome

JAMES T. FARMER III

———

Photography by

JEFF HERR

GIBBS SMITH

TO ENRICH AND INSPIRE HUMANKIND

Dedicated in loving memory to my grandfather, the

Reverend Doctor Napp N. Granade.

His life was a celebration of faith, family and love,

and for that legacy I am immeasurably blessed.

CONTENTS

FOREWORD

by DEBORAH ROBERTS

I don't exactly remember when I met James Farmer. I guess it really doesn't matter, because it seems we've always been friends. We are kindred Southern spirits. We like to find the good in things. We smile easily and endlessly. And we both cherish family and home.

Home is something James has spent many years exploring. As a homebody, he clearly understands what many of us do: that a house and a home are entirely different things.

That said, when James designs a home, he designs truly that—a home. Aside from his use of impeccably curated layers, colors and textures, James pulls from his roots to create a warm and lived-in aesthetic. It's not just how the Schumacher window treatments gracefully fall over the Thibaut grass cloth wallcoverings. Nor is it how a custom lampshade, a mohair sofa and your grandmother's crystal atop an antique sideboard make an eye-catching living room. It's how each its own creates beauty, but together they make you feel connected to your roots.

In this beautifully illustrated book, James shows us what it means to be at home. To come home. Wherever that might be. From the sights. To the smells. To the feelings that bubble up inside us just thinking of it, we experience the joy and beauty of home.

Though I've lived in New York City for the past thirty years, I am deeply and happily still a Georgia girl. On any given day, my thoughts wander back to my early years in Perry, Georgia, the same quaint and sweet patch of beauty that James wants to never leave.

The word *home* holds a tremendous amount of power for me. It reminds me of all the things that made me the woman I am today. The nurturing. The loving. The living.

My childhood home wasn't fancy. In fact, it was quite ordinary. A small, unremarkable, four-bedroom ranch-style house, where nine kids managed to grow up feeling close and connected in an unpolished part of town. We had one bathroom, a small kitchen and less than an acre of property. But my parents couldn't have been prouder of our home. Mom planted begonias and geraniums after each Georgia winter and worried over her azalea bush. This modest home was the one she never had as a child.

But it's not just the physical place that is seared in my memory. It's also the aroma of Mama's chicken and dressing along with her famous peach cobbler. I can still smell that potent blend of southern culinary magic that filled the house for days.

Home, for me, calls to mind that warm, cozy feeling of being loved, fed and cherished.

Many of my siblings and I have made new lives far away from Georgia. But when we speak of home, we all instinctively know that it means Perry. That little house is still right there, still calling out to us though it's empty now.

My current home is far bigger and more elaborate than the one I grew up in. And I must confess that I don't make a delectable homemade dessert. But I have worked hard to create my own traditions and enduring memories, which I hope my family will hold onto in mind and spirit. The rich aroma of my cherished coffee brewing each morning. The sound of my husband's sizzling chicken dinner in the oven. The fragrant smells of a roaring fire in the fireplace in winter and of a Virginia fir Christmas tree each December.

On these pages you will see that home means something different to each of us. For some, it is about childhood and those memories stored while growing up. But for many of us, home isn't a location. It's a feeling deep down in our souls. It's that place you go to emotionally when you're feeling low or going through a tough experience. If you're lucky, you'll realize in those moments that home is what makes us feel whole. In *Arriving Home*, James shows us exactly why that feeling of home is so important. It's not just about the beautiful spaces he creates. Instead, he shows us that a home, whether new or old, lived in or fresh, is about the feeling you have and hold onto when you're there.

INTRODUCTION

. . . And I hope, by Thy good pleasure,

Safely to arrive at home.

—ROBERT ROBINSON, FROM *COME THOU, FOUNT OF EVERY BLESSING, CA 1758*

These lyrics, found in the hymn "Come Thou Fount of Every Blessing," ring ever so true. Is there a better feeling than arriving home? Whether a long journey sets us homeward, or perhaps returning from a day's work, an intangible feeling evokes and, in turn, engages our senses as the approach toward home becomes illuminated by the tangible.

We see our home and visually note the aesthetics and pleasantries of the colors and materials; we feel the doorknob in our palm, warmed by the sun or chilled by the cold; we smell the comforts of fresh laundry or supper on the stove, followed by the taste of said supper. We hear the door creak open and shut softly and have a peace that only arriving home affords.

In the Southern pantheon of homes, there is a gracious plenty of styles, genres and sizes shaping the heritage of our region into a notable neck of the woods of enough merit that our cities and towns are very specific destinations for travelers. People journey to see our homes past and present, eat our food and stroll through our gardens. As tourists, house hunters, astute architectural scholars and history buffs, their insight and curiosity take them to towns like Eufaula, Alabama, for "The Pilgrimage," a tour of homes and raison d'etre for towns

like Eufaula, rich in architectural specimens. Savannah, Charleston, St. Francisville, Beaufort and Beaufort (pronounced differently), Thomasville, Madison, Fairhope and Point Clear, Baton Rouge and Shreveport, and the neighborhoods within larger towns and cities too, all represent pearls strung on a southerly strand.

In turn, we Southerners are a "house proud" people. We devote generations of time and dedicate inheritances and annual income to our homes and gardens, and we open them for weddings, parties, family gatherings and community events. It is not a brash type of pride, but a wholesome sense of duty to share and include our friends and family for life's events in an intimate setting—a true reflection of our hospitality. We set the tone for arriving home not only for ourselves but for our people. I refer to our hallmark sense of hospitality and style as "unapologetic." We confidently mix heirlooms with contemporary art, set our tables with generations of silver and store-bought finds, serve garden vegetables on fine china, and pluck whatever is blooming in the yard to arrange in julep cups. As college students we wear our Sunday best to football games. As Southerners, our style does not warrant an apology for blending the old with the new, the common with the fine or the familial with the found; our style is simply reinforced with confidence stamped on our culture. After all, that's the way mama did it too.

As an interior designer, my task is taking the leap on our clients' behalf to make a house into a home. I have written and spoken about this topic for a number of years. A house is a structure—an architectural dwelling providing shelter from the elements. A home tugs at one's heartstrings. Emotions, senses and memories are fibers spun into threads, woven into the fabric that dresses our lives. As my dear friend Jane Kathryn Evans in Memphis says, "We are old souls; we just know how our mothers and grandmothers felt and keep that feeling going for the next generation." She first told me this in our twenties, and that gift of being an old soul at a young age allows those of us in the design field to borrow from that past, revere, and restore it for the next generations.

At my design firm, we are tasked with setting and providing the backdrop of our clients' lives much like a stage designer or set decorator does for a play or movie. The design of the banister and runner selected for the stairs was thought through years before the prom photos are taken. The front door material and color were customized long before Christmas card poses are taken and mailed to family and friends. As our clients settle and snuggle into sofas, the very hand of the velvet appointed to the upholstery was contemplated as to whether a cottony blend, linen weave or silk-thread velvet would be a better suit.

The layers of flooring, floor covering, wall materials and coverings, lighting, plumbing fixtures and trim must be acknowledged while the house is being framed, for studs are needed to support paneling, valves need to be in place for pipes, and wiring has to be run before the chandelier illuminates Thanksgiving dinner. This aspect of design is one of the difficult ones to parlay, because clients and those awaiting the results may find it difficult to comprehend the steps beforehand. Before that warm water can wash over your hands from the beautiful faucet, it must be plumbed. I often say that plumbing fixtures are the jewelry of the bathroom; before that jewel or metal can shine, it must be mined!

Many folks never realize the depth and breadth these decisions of paint, flooring, materials and furnishings have on our psyches. Whether you are walking through an airport or into your home, a deliberate design decision has been made—for good or bad—and sets the tone. Hiring and trusting a professional is a service and gift to oneself; whether it is a designer or electrician, their services allow you to focus on the other elements of your life. Though my mother had lovely taste, she worked with professionals to help set the tone and structure of our home, which then allowed her personal touches, such as photographs, artwork and a hospitable personality, to shine. The essence of my job, then, is to allow my clients' best selves to shine in their homes.

As we tour homes across the country, I hope the common thread seen is not how well a room cleans up for a photograph, but how each room glows from within. The ability to host a family gathering, a cocktail party, or the reading of the Saturday-morning paper or a good book—all with a gracious dose of Southern charm, personality and style—is the task at hand for our designs. I am ever so thankful that this challenge is my occupation. The privilege of serving wonderful clients—especially with my team—is a blessing.

As we like to say upon arrival at our homes, "Come on in, y'all."

OAK BOWERY, ALABAMA THE BEAUTIFUL

When I was at Auburn, many social events were held at the outlying older homes that had been converted into event venues over the years. Weddings and sorority formals became the mainstays of these antebellum and turn-of-the-century houses. One such place, Oak Bowery, set among oaks atop a gentle knoll, held a fond place in my mind. When my design team was contacted by a delightful young couple from Alabama to help them restore and design the "new" home they had purchased outside of Auburn, it was not until I looked out the window upon arrival that I realized we were at Oak Bowery!

The couple had engaged Norman Askins, a highly regarded architect from Atlanta, to design a carport and kitchen addition and some structural changes, so my design team got started with plumbing, lighting and color selection.

A mahogany secretary stands as sentinel in the foyer. The fretwork and yew wood banding give character and stylized personality to a traditional piece. I often paint the interior of secretaries and the like to show off their collected objects on display. A chinoiserie chair with an Italian Bargello pattern is a painterly complement to the wooden English case piece. The transom was inspired by caning patterns often seen on chairs.

We went with a soft creamy white for the body of the home and deep muddy green barely a shade above black for the shutters. We used as much antique and reclaimed brick as possible. Classic plantings of boxwood, hydrangea, camellia and magnolia drift among new fencing, driveways and lawns, creating some order to a once more conjuncted and intersected style of landscape.

Keeping the center-hall floor plan intact, the foyer became the largest room, serving as the gateway, spillway and corridor to all parts of the home. Off the foyer are the study, dining room, guest room and family room, respectively, keeping the center-hall, four-room "up and down" plan in place and allowing for additions such as the modern kitchen and bathrooms to be placed accordingly.

We were able to reinforce, preserve and reuse much of the heart pine from the original home. The family room walls, which had been covered with decades of plaster and paper, once again glow in a deep honey tone and strike a lovely contrast with the lighter tones in the guest room across the foyer.

Rooting the design scheme of a home in what is tried and true allows the design to remain timeless rather than trendy. I'm not the first or the last designer to paint an antebellum house with white columns, but I can select a color that is a workhorse for the ages. Is it the right creamy base? How does the hue change with the seasons? What foliage and vegetation surround the home, and how do their greens reflect and enhance the color? Answering these kinds of questions leads to lasting selections for such projects—not only the paint colors but the essence of style. Purposeful and proper decisions made on behalf of the home ensure its viability into the next century. Good design is a gift to our future.

All around the grounds, classic plantings of boxwood, hydrangea, camellia and magnolia drift among new fencing, driveways and lawns, creating some order to a once more conjuncted and intersected style of landscape.

ABOVE LEFT: The transoms in the home were designed by my team, inspired by caning seen on an antique chair bottom.

ABOVE RIGHT AND OPPOSITE: The foyer's original horizontal paneling was painted Benjamin Moore "Linen White," with moldings and ceilings a shade darker, more reflective of putty. This allows a neutral vein to course the center of the home and lets all-stars such as antiques, Persian rugs and artwork shine.

ABOVE: An antique alabaster lamp and ivory-glazed garden stool add crispness to the masculine hues of this room. One entire wall is devoted to built-ins complete with hunting trophies, antique books and waterfowl prints—all lit by library sconces. The wool plaid is by Colefax and Fowler.

RIGHT: For the study, I wanted to create a true retreat as well as home office. Grass cloth woven with a tobacco-hued raffia thread is applied above the pine paneling. The mantel is original to the home. The mocha, burnt sienna and teal colorway of the Schumacher hunting dog linen at the windows and on the pillow at left was the inspirational fabric; its colors are seen in the velvet, leather and wool plaid used elsewhere in the room. The painting is by my Auburn friend Emily York Ozier (EMYO). A faded Persian carpet is atop a sisal rug for added texture and handsome layers.

A British tradition I have adopted is choosing a dining room wall color that reflects the warm hues found in candlelight, for the reason that it complements the complexion of those dining. Soft peaches, ambers, apricots and persimmon shades glow with candlelight.

OPPOSITE AND ABOVE: To ground the room, I chose an English pine huntboard as a serving piece. This is a nod to Southern homes of this period and the South's heritage as an English colony. The Italian chinoiserie-style painted leather screen is fabulous against the apricot Farrow and Ball strié paper. Chinoiserie, English antiques and serving pieces of varying genres add to the collected feel of the room. Another English tradition borrowed here is the apricot hue of the room, whereas English dining rooms often are painted or papered in this color family. My team designed the transoms and crown molding to return some architectural prowess to the home.

ABOVE AND RIGHT: The family room's heart pine walls, which had been covered with decades of plaster and paper, once again glow in a deep honey tone. Greens and blues in the study balance the color scheme of the adjacent dining room extremely well. The oil above the mantel is by South Carolina artist Millie Gosch. East Alabama and the Low Country both boast terrific sunsets of which Gosch's work is fondly reminiscent.

LEFT AND ABOVE: For the kitchen, Alabama white marble serves as the countertops, as heart pine does for the island top and all the kitchen flooring—honed but not polished. The mix of marble, tile and wood creates a kitchen for solid working and entertaining, while the fabrics and furniture soften windows and seating. I love to bend the rules with traditional "all-white" kitchens and add pops of color with the island and runners.

LEFT AND ABOVE: A suite of Schumacher fabrics and wall coverings give zest to the kitchen with fresh colorways of classic patterns. The "Zanzibar" trellis is freshly printed in a vibrant green and pairs with the iconic "Citrus Garden" on the shades. The artwork is an antique piece of hand-painted wallpaper. Portuguese majolica-style roosters are now lamps. The dove gray low boy is a solid neutral for this colorful space.

ABOVE: For the niche at the upper landing, Italian lamps and a French commode are paired against a vintage mirror that reflects the artwork on the stairwell.

RIGHT: Floral artwork by Alabama artist Andrew Lee leads cheerfully up the stairs. The upper floor echoes the layout below, with a wide center hall and four rooms congruently serving as bedrooms.

OPPOSITE: For the master suite, I mixed handsome and pretty shades of pearly blues, grays and taupe. Pops of color are seen in the lamps and artwork. The bed is handmade by Andrew Reid.

ABOVE: The original fireplaces throughout the home were restored to working order and serve as architectural reminders of their purpose but also as beautiful mantelpieces for decor and visual interest.

ABOVE AND OPPOSITE: Old homes lack contemporary bathrooms and kitchens, so we often take other spaces and create new bathrooms, in particular. Architect Normal Haskins drew a new bathroom for each bedroom. Here, soothing tones of brown, white marble and a fireplace create the ultimate master bathroom with old-school charm.

OPPOSITE: Southern porches are nostalgic. Here, classic sentiment is captured with Brumby rockers and a bed swing, potted plants and a "haint" blue ceiling. Modern comforts such as zippy outdoor pillows, a television and fans make this outdoor space a wonderful destination.

ABOVE: An antique hooked rug, shades of cream and white, and pops of teal and citrine create a soothing guest suite. Artist Lauren Dunn painted the home's vivid portrait seen above the mantel.

SOUTHWARD TO CONNECTICUT

For a young family in New York City, a country home in Connecticut became a weekend retreat from the hustle and bustle of the city. Being from North Carolina originally, the wife and mother of this household fondly recalled her childhood home as inspiration for her new one. Her mother joined us at our initial meeting in Connecticut, and quickly this gaggle of displaced Southerners began making small-town connections and networking our even smaller southerly world. I love witnessing Southerners in a city like New York or being part of a throng of us out of our native geography; we are swift to connect maiden names and down-the-line cousins, but the subject of houses, homes, gardens and familial silver effervescently bubbles to the top of the conversation.

A Philip Jeffries striped raffia grass cloth in the entry hall is trimmed and bordered with a Schumacher Greek key tape—emphasizing the room's moldings and architectural pizazz. The freshly papered space give antiques with provenance, such as a handsome mahogany secretary, porcelains and artwork, the ability to shine.

The couple were keen on having the warmth and collected feel of a Southern home, set amid the gorgeous mountains and verdant landscape of Connecticut's Litchfield County. The house has all the aspects of a rambling country home with just the right amount of polish. To me, this is the essence of Southern style: ramble and polish, mixing the high and the low, the fine with the everyday. Notably, our quintessential style is hallmarked by our unapologetic combination of heirlooms with contemporary styles, creating layers of curated and collected pieces that tell a story. And next to our hospitality and homes, a good story is quite the trademark for us too.

Some of my favorite rooms in a home are not necessarily those that are grand or significant in scale, but ones that serve as hyphens, niches, connectors and links joining additions, wings or rooms. The niche in this home serves as vestibule between the foyer and living room but has architectural charm with great arches and windows. With a wide gallery and foyer, this home opens up like a chapter of a great book.

The dining room is an homage to country homes and English tradition. As a traditionalist, I usually follow the formula of table, chairs, serving pieces, etc., yet my creative side pushes the envelope to break the rules just a bit. I wished to take the "formal" aspect away from this dining space but allow proper furnishings to still hold their place. Gorgeous, classic and always in style, a mix of brown or wood furniture always has its place. This base allowed me to springboard into other finishes and styles and mix genres, for a lovely effect. The walls are clad in a perfectly peach grass cloth, giving depth and texture to the walls in that British tradition of dining room colorways, while the ceiling is lacquered in a rich green—smooth and inky against the grass cloth for congruent complementing.

In formal living rooms, as with dining rooms, I love to adhere to the formality of appropriate, formulaic furniture placement yet bend that rule for how we live today. A favorite arrangement of mine is placing two small sofas perpendicular to the fireplace wall and a larger sofa anchoring an opposite wall and flanked by two chairs. This allows for gracious amounts of seating and traffic flow while also creating niches for conversation among a group of folks or intimate enough for a couple of guests.

ABOVE: Schumacher "Hydrangea Drape" in a neutral colorway gives the eye vertical interest up the stairway.

OPPOSITE: Lee Jofa "Hollyhock" is seen in handsome contrast with nailhead trim on lattice-back chairs. A Scottish oil painting of a moor in bloom with heather carries the soft hues of the fabric.

ABOVE: The windowed niches on either side of the entryway have just the right amount of space for vignettes complete with demilunes, lamps and lovely wall treatments.

RIGHT: The foyer is the gateway to the study, dining room and living room and allows each of these rooms to shine. Glimpses are advantageous from this great vantage point and corridor.

OVERLEAF: Leather and plaid, pottery and china, wood paneling and chinoiserie meld together in a cozy concoction of handsomeness and comfort—but with just the right amount of shimmer from the lacquered ceiling to make this gentleman's study glow.

OPPOSITE: The pine-paneled study is a working office and gentleman's retreat. Red glazed pottery from North Carolina harkens to the wife's family's heritage, while the figurines on the shelves from Madagascar nod to the husband's family business there. Mixing handsome and feminine elements creates a harmonious cadence in rooms.

ABOVE: The signature fabric depicts camellias—a Southern signature flower—and recalls the homes and gardens throughout the South that boast this loveliest of blossoms.

A custom mahogany and ebonized dining table serves as the center point of the room. A sisal and wool diamond-pattern rug grounds the space and gives an earthen element and pattern repetition with the trellis-backed chairs. Repeating pattern on different planes creates wonderful cadence in a room.

ABOVE: The same plaid as the chairs is pleated for the lampshades on the bamboo billiard-style light fixture—another twist on tradition, for the expected crystal chandelier is not seen here.

RIGHT: A stunning antique sideboard in a finish similar to but not matching the dining table helps commands attention.

OPPOSITE: Cerulean blue glass lamps, green-and-white-plaid shades and custom pressed botanicals keep the room verdant and vibrant, even on the coldest of winter days in Connecticut.

PREVIOUS OVERLEAF: For the kitchen, we were able to open the space to serve as a multifunctional room for cooking, dining and sitting. Using pops of white—with the nearly white marble, trim, barstools, background of the paper and fabric and in accessories—gives the kitchen a fresh vibe. I often combine stone and wood for countertops.

ABOVE LEFT:. Wallpaper from Thibaut in a small trellis pattern adds visual texture without competing with the tactile textures of wood, stone and fabric.

ABOVE RIGHT:. The large room is dressed in green, sage and light blue for continuity throughout, including the exaggerated ticking sofa fabric.

OPPOSITE: The wife's family table from her childhood home in North Carolina now hosts her family in Connecticut. A Sanderson toile is used on the windows.

ABOVE: Details and textures in the furnishings and fabrics contrast with the lacquering of the antique screen. The mix of handsome pieces in a formal living room is one way to keep a seemingly "formal" room more approachable and not dainty or uncomfortable.

RIGHT: Anchoring the larger sofa wall is a coromandel screen, complete with gold, ivory and jade highlights depicting everyday life in a Chinese village. This touch of whimsy in the subject matter of a more formal piece is part of the rhythm of mixing styles and patterns and pieces to form harmony in design. Two lattice-patterned club chairs add colorful touches.

A pair of sofas clad in a Cowtan and Tout "Treasure Flower" provide bold pattern and set the color palette. Oranges, greens, ivory, tobacco and ebony make what is often thought of as a dainty, more feminine room into a handsome place for reading, cocktails or family gatherings. Here, a creamy ochre grass cloth is backdrop for Asian, Italian and French antiques, while a putty-hued lacquered ceiling reflects and refracts daylight, candlelight or lamplight. An antique family heirloom Oushak carpet gives a softer palette underfoot, mimicking the bolder hues above. Over the mantel, a Venetian harbor scene brings the room's colors to the fireplace wall.

OPPOSITE: Bookshelves are backed in a Twigs pheasant-patterned paper, which serves as the perfect backdrop for literary displays, collections and objets d'art.

ABOVE: A bayed niche with doors opening into the garden is framed by panels of Cowtan and Tout "Rapolo" linen and emerald jade jars—harkening the green outdoors.

RIGHT: In the living room, Italian pieces—a commode and Murano lamps—serve as foundational and illuminating accents for a familial chinoiserie mirror.

OVERLEAF: The sunroom, next to the living room, is light and cheerful enough for summertime use but cozy enough for the coldest of days. A television and fireplace provide for both binge-watching and ambiance. A custom velvet sectional is tucked into the corner, while tiger-patterned slipper chairs provide extra seating. Foliage and fronds are printed on the raffia-toned grass cloth.

OPPOSITE: The powder room paper by Thomas Strahan is called "Farmer." A cheerful Brunschwig and Fils fabric on the shade, yellow light fixture and artwork give the room generous personality.

ABOVE LEFT: A downstairs guest room's walls are treated in a printed grass cloth. One of my favorite tricks of the trade is using a printed pattern on grass cloth, for it gives pattern and texture to otherwise flat walls.

ABOVE RIGHT: The daughter's bedroom is a suite of blushes and pinks, offset with a blue trellis paper and peachy pink ceiling. Georgia artist Darby Boruff botanicals crown the headboard.

ABOVE LEFT: A suite of soft aqua shades, greens and tans strike a balance for feminine flair and handsome suitability. An antique secretary provides a place for study or writing notes. Colefax and Fowler "Snowtree" is the pattern on the walls.

ABOVE RIGHT: Bullion fringe, nailheads and tufting add details to the upholstery pieces that make up the sitting area of this suite. An embroidered Brunschwig and Fils check dresses the windows.

OPPOSITE: Touches of hand-painted artistry are seen in the chinoiserie chests that flank the bed and the coffee table. Erika Powell fabrics were used to make the lampshades. A custom bed, monogrammed linens and silver-framed family photos make the room truly personal.

A
LAKESIDE
RETREAT

For clients looking for a nearby weekend getaway from Atlanta, Lake Oconee is the perfect distance. These clients bestowed one of the highest honors a client can give: entrusting their designer with not only their primary home but their second home as well. In these longstanding working relationships, personality, collections, sentiments and style all merge. At the helm with his wonderful architectural plans was Greg Busch. Rhett Bonner and his construction team took Greg's vision and brought it to life, allowing our designs to further develop and for us to confidently furnish the project.

Set among hardwoods and pines, the house is nestled on a quiet shore of the lake, with expansive views of the water. The home had been enjoyed by the family and friends for years, but the incredible view was not truly taken advantage of, nor the floor plan suited for a growing family with grandchildren and cousins being added. Greg took the shell of the house and

A fabulous view of the water from the living room was gained when the back of the house was opened up. An Elizabeth Eakins plaid rug anchors this room and dining room too, which is open to the living room. Mixed upholstery—plaids, velvet and leather—will all wear with time and keep the sitting room comfortable.

opened the back to create a masterful opportunity to take in the water with steel and glass floor-to-ceiling windows. Decking became porches, and more interior square footage and a more adequate flow lent to a very desirable floor plan. With the topography sloping toward the lake, the upper floor boasts the master suite and main living and dining rooms and kitchen, while the terrace level has room to host several families. Whether it's only a couple of folks or twenty, the house lends well to weekends spent here, Fourth of July parties and holidays too.

A large entryway, which used to have a choppy layout of foyer, stairwell and reading area, is now a welcoming entry and serves as an additional dining space for large parties.

By pushing out the living area into previous deck space, the house and lake become better acquainted. Sofas and chairs are centered on the fireplace, and nearly all take in the view through the spectacular windows. White horizontal paneling clads the walls and is repeated on the ceiling, letting the reclaimed beams' patina stand out.

The dining room, with a breathtaking view to the porch and on to the lake, can seat a crowd at the Italian monastery table. A woven raffia covers the walls, and the ceiling wears a faint icy blue, echoing the Southern tradition of porch ceilings being painted blue.

The new and improved kitchen is an expanded galley style that works beautifully for serving a crowd. Cherry butcher block is the countertop material, while a mix of brass and brushed nickel hardware, lighting and plumbing fixtures creates a nice mix. A vertical beaded paneled wall treatment, Shaker-style paneled cabinets and efficient millwork shores up the simple but noteworthy architecture of the space.

For the master bedroom and adjoining study, a soothing sage green is applied to the vertical, V-groove paneling. Complementary khaki, French blue and white further keep the palette refreshing.

A completely refurbished and rearranged master bath now provides a luxurious element to the master suite. Custom cabinetry serves as vanities, and the blue buffalo check harkens back to the bedroom. Oil paintings of the Dutch Low Country and an antique secretary bring in the antique elements every room needs—even a newly remodeled bathroom.

A chalky white Italian credenza is layered with pottery lamps, creamware, stacked oils and antique fish prints. The textures and layers of whites, creams, chalk and ochre makes for a soothing vignette.

ABOVE: We carried the raffia and creamy tones of the foyer into the living room with antiques and artwork, such as this wall anchored by the white Italian credenza. Charlie West pottery lamps sport Bunny Williams lampshades.

RIGHT: In the entryway, an antique French cherry oval table occupies the center of the room, serving as a "roundabout" of sorts, directing guests to different parts of the house. Antique chests in pine and bleached oak, antique landscapes and a new Chippendale-style railing further fill the space, which is wrapped in a tone-on-tone raffia grass cloth. The new door and its cheery color are complemented by the antique Oushak rug.

LEFT: The living room opens off the entryway and has seating arrangements that entice good old-fashioned conversation. Pottery, artwork and leatherbound books fill the built-in shelves.

ABOVE: A classic brick fireplace, antiques and a chalky Italian credenza add patinas to the room.

PREVIOUS OVERLEAF AND OPPOSITE: In the dining room, a bold pattern of lotuses and lily pads is complemented with a green plaid on the chairs and lampshades. The handmade iron light fixture was inspired by marsh grasses.

ABOVE: The sideboard is an antique French enfilade with a wonderful verdigris patina.

ABOVE: Linen white cabinetry in the kitchen includes open shelving, where displays of majolica and pottery add blended color.

RIGHT: An antique French draper's table serves as the kitchen island. Tribal runners ground the space.

ABOVE AND OPPOSITE: For the master bedroom, a
soothing sage green is applied to the vertical,
V-groove paneling. Complementary khaki, French
blue and white further keep the palette refreshing.
A leopard-print fabric emboldens the bamboo stool,
which serves a cheery role holding bedtime reading
selections.

OPPOSITE: A custom vanity brings luxury to the master bath, while symmetrical placement of accessories balances the space on both sides of the oval window.

ABOVE LEFT: A tone-on-tone British wallpaper from Lewis and Wood softly complements the marble field tile and border. The bleached-finished secretary with a fretwork façade stores bath salts, towels and an assortment of objet d'art.

ABOVE RIGHT: A soaker tub provides a place of respite after a long day on the lake. Oil paintings and a chandelier add to the feeling of luxury.

LEFT: The lower terrace level of the home has a large living area for watching sports or movies or playing games.

ABOVE: Additional bedrooms provide a warm and cozy space for family and friends.

PREVIOUS OVERLEAF AND ABOVE: The lower terrace proper is a combination of areas suited for napping, conversation and outdoor dining. White wicker, outdoor fabrics in fun patterns, rattan and potted plants make this the perfect destination. A hybrid of indoors and out, this deeply shaded porch serves as the midway point between the house and lake.

OPPOSITE: A dining porch complete with a grill and large table and chairs becomes a favorite perch to dine alfresco and take in the view. Mixes of wicker, rattan, wood and metal can be seen. The ceiling is a pickled cypress and the floor is "porch blue," in a fun flip-flop of Southern style.

A PLACE
TO CALL HOME
IN TOWN

For our clients' home in town, we were privileged to work with Greg Busch and his team for the architecture and then see those plans executed by Rhett Bonner and his crew. A bit more polished and buttoned up, this home has the façade of a town house but the feel of a cottage too, with mixed materials of terra-cotta tile, brick and stone. Set in a lovely wooded neighborhood very close to the hubbub of metro Atlanta, this home is a retreat for our clients and their family.

As the interior designers, we were tasked with the finishes and furnishings. Whether hosting their family or a large gathering of friends or coworkers, this couple entertains often and generously. I wanted the welcoming feeling these clients bestow on all those they encounter to be reflected in their home while retaining an elegance.

A mix of English, French and Italian antiques fill out the foyer with patina and provenance.

The enfilade of rooms is linked visually through a cased opening, which set a tone for rhythm and repetition in a most positive and delightful way when furnishing and designing the interiors. Pairs of demilunes, chests, chairs, lamps and mirrors flank architectural spaces with symmetry. Accessories balance the proportion with personality, as does artwork.

The foyer is a classic example of cadence and architectural scale working together harmoniously. The ochre-hued paper is backdrop for antique furnishings and serves as the neutral thread to pull from for the other wall treatments seen off the foyer.

The living room has copious seating in comfortable fabrics. Mixes of velvet and leather beckon people to sit by the fire or sink into a leather chair with a book or cocktail. Balanced and symmetrical furniture placement is relaxed by the tiger-print pattern and hand-blocked linen pillows. The deep green coromandel screen behind the main sofa served as a springboard for the colors seen throughout the home and is balanced by the Scottish landscape over the limestone mantel. Steel and glass French doors lead to the garden, and the same arched opening is repeated on the other side, leading into the sunroom.

Large steel and glass doors and window separate the dining room from the terrace. The lively fabric selections give this space a conservatory-meets-dining room feel.

The sunroom doubles as a family room. Green sofas and cozy club chairs provide ample seating, while a framed antique textile sets the tone for the room's colorway. The garden and pool terrace can be seen through the doors and windows. Reclaimed beams, ceiling planks, bookshelves and an antique Irish coffee table add the wooden elements that balance the stone, steel and glass.

Kitchens can become filled with harder finishes like stone and metal. Here, architectural cabinetry hides appliances and allows the range and its hood to be focal points. White Carrera marble anchors the island, but softer elements like woven barstools and fabrics serve as counterpoints to the stone. The dark-stained wood floors are layered with tribal runners, and the stain is echoed on the beams above.

In the master bedroom, a calming palette of honey, indigo, camel and teal set the tone. The walls are upholstered in a camel's hair color of wool. An icy blue lacquered ceiling adds a touch of polish and glam. Monogrammed Matouk bedding, books, artwork and antiques add to the personal layers and familial touches in this room.

A hand-painted paper by George Spencer Designs creates vertical interest on the walls and leads the eye upward in the stairwell.

PREVIOUS OVERLEAF: In the living room, an arrowroot woven paper on the walls stands in complementary juxtaposition to a lacquered ceiling complete with fretwork pattern we designed. Schumacher "Persian Lancer" on the pillows pulls its colorway from the coromandel screen and dots the room with accents of coral, green, lapis and persimmon.

ABOVE: The wall opposite the bookcase, which opens to the dining room, is flanked with Louis Philippe chests, ivory and wood mirrors and antique pressed botanicals.

RIGHT: A large bookcase the clients found on a trip fits snugly into a niche. Opposite that wall is the opening to the dining room.

PREVIOUS OVERLEAF: The dining room walls are covered in "Adam's Eden" by Lewis and Wood. A pale French blue lacquered ceiling reflects the room below in near mirror-like perfection. Caned-back chairs along with upholstered-back host and hostess chairs can easily be moved into the adjoining living room for after-dinner conversation. Colors from the antique Mahal rug are seen throughout the room.

OPPOSITE: Christopher Spitzmiller lamps in emerald silk shades are a handsome complement to the chinoiserie sideboard. A stately octagonal gilt mirror reflects the room from its perch within the sideboard's niche.

ABOVE: An iron-and-glass console set against the window serves as additional serving and display space for silver. Papier-mâché geraniums by artist Livia Cetti add a touch a whimsy and softness to the vignette.

In the kitchen, a banquette and custom table with chairs are upholstered in a Lewis and Wood print. Contemporary artwork is a lovely contrast with a large antique framed set of botanicals.

PREVIOUS OVERLEAF: Forest green, deep turquoise and mustard yellow are found through the family room/sunroom. An antique Serapi rug brings the colors underfoot.

ABOVE: Paul Schneider lamps pick up the deep turquoise seen in the rug and artwork and is carried with the pillows and ottomans as well. Reclaimed beams, ceiling planks, bookshelves and an antique Irish coffee table add the wooden elements that balance the stone, steel and glass.

OPPOSITE: A pair of chairs flanking the fireplace are covered in a GP & J Baker velvet depicting colorful pheasants, and it is repeated on pillows too. A French oil depicting a loving mother and her sons is apropos over the carved limestone mantelpiece set against whitewashed bricks.

PREVIOUS OVERLEAF: In the master bedroom, an ikat pattern tester in a warm sepia tone drapes the bed niche—a handsome complement to the deep teal velvet headboard and foot bench. The red in the antique Mahal rug is a perfect field underfoot and plays off the colors found elsewhere in the room.

ABOVE: Built-ins opposite the bed host a collection of antique books, pottery and art. They flank a paneled wall and dark-stained credenza that hides the television.

OPPOSITE: Monogrammed Matouk bedding adds another touch of luxury.

ABOVE AND RIGHT: For the guest room, Brunschwig and Fils "La Tavera" in a neutral colorway dresses the walls and slopes. Antique pressed botanicals, white pottery lamps and white bedding keep the neutrality in check but also support pops of apple green gingham, raspberry red monogramming and powdery blue enfilade. A vintage wingback chair had the perfect frame for a colorful flame-stitch upholstery.

ABOVE AND RIGHT: Janus et Cie custom outdoor furniture holds center stage on the outdoor terrace. Perennials fabrics withstand the elements and provide comfortable seating for the lounging and dining areas. The bluestone is set as large pieces in an exaggerated running bond pattern then repeated on a different scale with the cobblestones. Hedging, flowers and a fountain soften the terrace's hardscape designed by Rick Ellis.

STATELY OAKS

For a young family in an old house, my team and I were tasked with making that juxtaposition work—revering the history and story of an older home, yet setting it against the modernity of a family's need.

First and foremost—the kitchen. Kitchens were dependencies to older homes, and when they were brought inside the house during the twentieth century, they were utilitarian at best. As we live today, the kitchen is the heartbeat of the home and typically open to the family living areas too. This proved to be true for this family in South Carolina. By rearranging some utilitarian space and adding a few feet to the square footage, we were able to give them a great place to cook and gather, and we even opened it up to a more spacious family room. I must admit, that within a minute or two of meeting a client for the first time, I'm often flailing my arms and gesturing

This home, while not antebellum in age, is reminiscent of the style with its classical portico and columns, white clapboard siding, black louvered shutters and gracious layers of green azaleas, boxwood and ferns. Jack awaits his next round of fetch.

how I would like to knock down walls within their home. It usually is a sign of my creative energy, but in this case it was a necessity to achieve the floor plan and desired result. By returning to a more traditional and formal layout, I was able to link the newer kitchen with the family room, dining room and sunroom. The dining room had been tucked away to the back of the house and thus was rarely used. By rearranging its placement with the study, we were then able to open the new dining room to the sunroom and family room, enabling a much closer proximity to the kitchen.

Traditional layouts just seem to fit and flow in older homes, and if walls could talk, they might have told us we went back to the original layout. White painted paneling, beautiful wallpaper and a color palette just close enough to a favorite football team's colors began to take shape. For the new dining room, a Zoffany paper in soft greens, apricots, creams and tans gave the once darker study a breath of fresh air. Heavier stained furniture pieces are expected in homes of this era, so a twist on that tradition was in painted furniture. A glazed white dining table, black fretwork chairs and a sisal rug keep the room a little more casual and renewed.

The sunroom had once been a porch and was enclosed sometime with the advent of air-conditioning. We were able to make the room into an extension of the family room and dining room with additional seating and dining space. The trim was painted out in a muddy sage green and the walls were left white, allowing the "haint" blue ceiling to pop.

The family room remains a major thoroughfare in this home. But with furniture placement and spacing, an ample seating area is centered on the fireplace, and thus a spacious "hallway" connects the family's entrance, kitchen and sunroom. Benjamin Moore "Linen White" gives the woodwork and trim an updated freshness, allowing the color to come through with furniture pieces and artwork. What once had been recessed built-ins are now the passages into the dining room.

The kitchen was the catalyst for this home's renovation. Our client wished for a place to cook and eat, with separate spaces for butler's pantry, laundry and a family entry. Often with older homes, the square footage is there; it just needs rearranging for today's standards. Taking in some existing space and adding only a nominal amount to the footprint, the kitchen opened into an inviting room. Shaker-style cabinet doors, furniture-detailed kickboards and the beadboard ceiling are all painted in a fresh coat of "Linen White," while the island's green adds contrast. The room is filled with light from a larger cased opening leading to the family room and two windows in addition to the boxed bay window.

The foyer's transom frames a lovely view into the dining room. In the foyer, striped wallpaper by Schumacher is enhanced by a pattern-on-pattern approach with the original vertical wainscoting. The lighting fixture by the Vaughan makes for a lovely statement. Architectural touches such as raising and matching the height of the cased openings throughout and adding a transom off the foyer brought the amazing scale of the home into play.

PREVIOUS OVERLEAF: In the dining room, shades rather than heavy window treatments adorn the window and allow sunlight to stream. Intentional and curated pieces, such as the French still life over the mantel and the English bowfront chest speak to tradition. The relocated dining room now opens into the sunroom and to the family room through passages flanking the fireplace.

OPPOSITE: Italian majolica lamps stand the test of time as classic accoutrements while not being stuffy or too formal for this young family's aesthetic.

For the sunroom, I wanted to retain those elements that have served as hallmarks of Southern porches, such as rattan, wicker and "haint" blue on the ceiling, which is repeated on the wicker table. Indoor/outdoor fabrics by Carleton V and a Peter Dunham fig leaf pattern meld with woven furniture pieces. A stack of antique oil paintings, a tone-on-tone Oushak rug in olive and sage, and seasonal plants and flowers add texture and layers to the room. Opening onto the dining room and family room, the sunroom serves a dual purpose as additional seating and dining spaces.

ABOVE AND OPPOSITE: One end of the sunroom is furnished with a table and chairs to serve as overflow from the adjacent dining room, a place to play cards or put together a puzzle or to finish homework with a view onto the garden. I like an element of black to visually weight a room, and it serves as a classic accent among neutral or colorful compilations.

OPPOSITE: The family room sofas are covered in a deep persimmon channel-quilted velvet. Hand-blocked pillows in "Nympheus" by Lee Jofa (also seen on the Roman shade) and a wool plaid in coordinating colors add handsome touches. White pottery lamps by Charlie West light the room. Botanicals flank a Louis Philippe mirror, which reflects the room beautifully.

ABOVE: A striking French *buffet à deux corps* provides storage for games and books and anchors one end of the room. The various patterns in the room pull out colors that are complementary. The wall covering is a custom colorway by Quadrille.

ABOVE: The side table, collected objects, lamps and wall art work together as an intriguing vignette.

OPPOSITE: A Spanish trestle table with a sunburst trestle serves as the sofa table, echoing the pattern in the wallpaper.

OVERLEAF: A large, butcher block–topped island serves as the spillway and center point of the kitchen. Rattan barstools sport Schumacher "Lotus Garden," as do the shades and cafe curtain in the boxed bay niche.

OPPOSITE: The vertical, butt-jointed paneling and open shelves add a nostalgic touch along with the brass cupped pulls.

ABOVE LEFT: A cookbook niche is made intriguing with the addition of fun collectibles and candy jars set just high enough not to be within easy reach.

ABOVE RIGHT: A former passage and shallow pantry became a wet bar and additional pantry space. Mirth Studio tiles are seen on the backsplash, creating a lovely pattern and complement to the collection of imari and English painted plates.

SOHO FARMHOUSE

In New York City, "SoHo" and "NoHo" refer to southern and northern placement of Houston Street. In my county of the same name as the street, we refer to the southern and northern ends of the county as "SoHo" and "NoHo"—tongue in cheek, of course. And for the record, it is "House-ton" here as well as in the Big Apple.

For clients just north of Atlanta, the idea of a farmhouse and weekend getaway in "SoHo" was appealing. Here again, I'm referring to my home county in Georgia. Hunting, fishing and family gatherings set amidst longleaf pines, live oaks and pecan orchards became a reality as they built their lodge and began spending more time in this bucolic locale. My firm was tapped to help design and furnish this home, with respect to the history of the land and Southern hunting traditions but comfortable for everyday

A statement wall of brown-and-white English transferware is arranged with Black Forest mounts and pottery lamps and supported by a lowboy console. Views into the living room and dining room can be seen from the foyer.

use, wear and tear. Pine paneling, a mural-clad dining room, wool plaids, leather and English antiques have stood the test of time for Southern hunting farms, and I channeled that tradition for this project.

The foyer is a nod to the Fall Line—a geographic anomaly in our region, a watershed diverting rivers to the Gulf or Atlantic, respectively. Here palmettos begin to skirt pine trees and Spanish moss starts to drape the oaks. Palmetto and ferns are seen on the grass cloth in the foyer, which is finished with a pine-paneled ceiling, English brandy boards and hunt paintings. To correlate with the living room and dining room seen from here, I used handsome neutral hues of tobacco, raffia and mahogany.

The living room is divided up into two main seating areas and adjoins an additional pine-paneled parlor. I told my clients that I wanted this room to be dressed in "khakis and white shirt—suitable dress for any occasion but easily dressed up with a blazer and tie or relaxed with loafers." White horizontal paneling above the honey-toned pine wainscoting allows the artwork and accessories to shine. The pine woodwork is carried throughout the room and into the parlor too—adding continuity and handsome architecture reminiscent of South Georgia plantations. I love using complementary colors in varying degrees, such as deep orange and celadon green as opposed to primary red and green. It gives that sense of *je ne sais quois* to a room's palette.

For the parlor adjoining the living room, the walls are fully paneled in pine, as is the ceiling. With this warm backdrop, fabrics and furniture in shades of jade and forest green mix with darker wood antiques.

In the kitchen, I wanted to invoke the pine woodlands seen just beyond the lake. Pine needle–green cabinets and the knotty pine island mimic the woodwork in other rooms. The breakfast area includes an antique wood banquette that is sometimes called into service.

The dining room was my opportunity to pay homage to muraled dining rooms seen in England and reinterpreted in American colonies. Southern hunting plantations took inspiration from British hunting lodges and the result is a hybrid of both genres. Scenic papers give these rooms a story to tell. Formulaic furniture placements are noted, and the walls begin to inject personality and pizazz. For the seating, a set of "sheep bone," or "mutton leg," chairs are a weightier choice compared to, traditional dining chairs. A couple other complementary textures of note are the card-stock shades on a crystal chandelier as opposed to silk, and the sisal and wool rug as opposed to a more formal Persian rug. This further exemplifies the code of Southern style by mixing the high and the low, the common and the rare and the fine with the everyday—unapologetically.

This home has many bedrooms for the ever-expanding family. Suites with coordinating florals and plaid anchor either end of the house as well as the upper floor.

An Italian pier mirror reflects set above an English brandy board reflects hunt paintings across the way. A palmetto and fern wallpaper warms the entire entryway.

PREVIOUS OVERLEAF: The pine coffered ceiling seen in the living room is a classic canopy for Southern homes. Mossy green velvet and wool plaid sofas anchor the seating, while brass study lamps and overhead brass fixtures illuminate the room along with tea caddies turned into lamps. An antique painted leather screen serves as centerpiece of the back wall is flanked by antique prints of ducks and geese. A bronze sculpture of a hunting dog with his prize, contemporary lamps, and a mix of celadon and imari-style planters accessorize the back table.

ABOVE: A field trial canvas by Tennessee artist Emily York Ozier is left unframed above the mantel, lending a more casual element to the room.

RIGHT: The parlor, across from the living room, is warmed with wood paneling. Schumacher "Lotus Garden" is seen on the window, chairs and pillows.

ABOVE: Furniture in shades of jade and forest green complement the colors across the hall and further keep the parlor cozy.

OPPOSITE: A secretary, with mahogany and yew wood accents, displays part of the owner's collection of porcelain. Blue-and-white temple jars, plates and platters are the classic complement to pine paneling.

OPPOSITE: A wet bar serves as the connecting corridor between the kitchen and dining room. Its elliptical fretwork cabinets dress up the space between the more formal dining room and casual kitchen. Georgia marble, painted paneling and brass fixtures and fittings harmonize in this space.

ABOVE LEFT: Pine needle–green cabinets and the knotty pine island tie the kitchen to other rooms in the home. Honed Georgia marble serves as the perimeter countertops and backsplash. Copper lanterns light the island, and a vintage tribal runner spreads across the oak floor.

ABOVE RIGHT: In the breakfast room portion of the kitchen, horizontal boards are painted white, in keeping with other walls in the house, setting off pops of green from oyster plates, gingham curtains and artwork. An amber-hued heart pine table, a linear brass light fixture, a sisal rug and English oak chairs with rush bottoms create a suite of neutral tones.

OPPOSITE: Scenic wallpaper by Paul Montgomery depicts the Low Country, where pines and palms meet with wetlands and fields. Using darker wood pieces for the table and sideboard, colorful opportunities arose from the paper's palette. A rich green trims out the crown, while a misty greige caps the ceiling as a fog does on a pond. Rosy apricot velvet by Nancy Corzine covers mutton-leg side chairs and pulls out the sunset hues in the paper, while deep gray-green wool clads the end chairs completed with chunky nailheads.

ABOVE: Local gardener and "flower lady" Mary Royal supplied the dahlias, which I arranged in a white vessel. Mandarin ducks in a brilliant green add more color and whimsy to the room.

LEFT: Peacock blue glazed lamps with leafy silk shades frame the simple, rounded corners of a Louis Phillippe mirror while lighting a collection of silver, a blue-and-white charger and antique Chinese vases.

A tableau of brown and green, the master bedroom with Jacobean-style tester is lightened with Brandon Godwin–designed fabrics depicting Georgia bobwhite quail and longleaf pine boughs.

PREVIOUS OVERLEAF: Amber and tobacco serve as the colorways for a twin guest room. Jute in each bedroom is a soothing floor covering layered atop the dark, stained oak floors. A tribal Persian runner further adds to the layered look.

OPPOSITE: A Thibaut print depicting herons and grasses in a deep chocolate glaze is set against the aqua arrowroot wall covering. A "rice carved" mahogany bed is skirted in a caramel check.

ABOVE: Another play on blue and brown is punctuated with yellow pottery lamps. Mahogany and oak furniture contrast with watery blue woven sisal on the wall.

HOME AGAIN TO EVANGLEN

Longtime clients and friends decided to build a new home on their extraordinary farming operation. "I have never lived in a new house," said the husband. Having lived in older family homes, the idea of building a new house on the property became an anticipated chapter in this family's story.

We had worked with the couple to redecorate their previous home, as well as with their children on their homes, so my team was honored to continue this relationship. Taking inspiration from a setting amidst longleaf pines on a gentle slope with a view towards a duck pond, the home, too, rises like the pines from the Georgia red clay.

Antique materials were introduced into the home's construction elements to infuse it with some nostalgia of the family's older homes, giving it the gift of provenance. Old bricks reclaimed from nearby Macon, beams from barns

An English mahogany sideboard holds antique blue-and-white, including jars turned into lamps. Pops of green majolica plates and a beveled family heirloom mirror create a cheery entrance to the home.

and specimen boards of cypress and heart pine were integrated into the fiber of this home.

Twisting on tradition a bit, this new home took inspiration from French country elements, with steep gables, eyebrow arched windows and clerestory dormers. The layout is open enough from room to room but sectioned appropriately for demarcation, traffic flow, furniture placement and household tasks. Repurposing antique heirloom pieces from the original Evanglen was a gracious start.

The foyer greets people with a Chippendale-inspired fretwork railing whose idea came from an older porch railing at a nearby home. Framed prints from antique ornithology books create a grid of an architecture on the stairwell wall, while Grandmother's chandelier infuses the spirit of generations that came before into this home.

I believe it is important for a newer home's aesthetic to thoughtfully integrate materials and proportions that give nod to tradition and perhaps how a house grows and expands or changes with the generational shifts. Brick floors in the combination dining room and music room give the feel of a porch or terrace perhaps closed-in by a generation before.

The dining room is the cornerstone of this home— the main thoroughfare intentionally placed and appointed to serve as the dining room proper, but also the hyphen that connects the living, family and music rooms with the kitchen, foyer and bedrooms beyond. Updated upholstery around an antique table provides balance and bridges the old with the new.

A large living room with groups of seating arrangements absorbs the family as they gather. The adjacent family room flows from here and the kitchen, allowing the couple to relax on their own at the end of the day or easily with a larger group when the children and grandchildren are home. A Schumacher chintz on the windows was the inspiration for the color scheme, which is reflected in the grass cloth tones, the persimmon velvet sofa and accents of kiwi green. An Oushak rug in soft aquas, ruby, terra-cotta and mossy greens grounds the living room and allows the color scheme to continue on this plane. Shades of green, such as kiwi, olive and pine needle, meld with persimmon, apricot, peach and orange as they do in the Georgia landscape with red clay soil, pines, grasses and sunsets.

Kitchens often become the trendiest rooms in a home, and my take is to meld with modern technology but keep with tradition, rooting the kitchen in classic homeness and practical style. Georgia marble, butcher block countertops and stainless appliances are the workhorses of the kitchen, allowing lovely lighting, softer surfaces for colorful fabrics and other aesthetics to shine amidst the hustle and bustle of a modern kitchen.

The cypress-paneled study is a masculine retreat complete with red leather, taxidermy trophies and handsome plaid. A Schumacher windowpane plaid creates geometry and architecture at the large window, and an antique brass chandelier from the original home now sheds light in this new one.

A new chapter now unfolds for a family that had called the same place home for decades. The older home is now a family hunting lodge and will certainly be cherished for generations to come.

Framed prints from antique ornithology books create an architecture-like grid on the stairwell wall.

LEFT: A pecky cypress mantel, antique bricks at the fireplace surround, reclaimed beams and heart pine floors are the earthen elements in the living room, which serve in lovely contrast to the books, porcelains and furniture.

ABOVE: Two chairs in a Bunny Williams print for Lee Jofa balance a persimmon-hued tufted sofa in a Brunschwig and Fils velvet. The pine needle–green leather ottoman with nailheads doubles as a coffee table and additional seating too. Pecky cypress on the mantel and antique bricks on the fire surround add natural elements that echo the land and family farming heritage of peaches, pecans and timber.

OVERLEAF: Grass cloth and painted paneling complement one another as the backdrop for multicolor chintz and other sumptuous fabrics. Blue-and-white porcelain, green majolica and antique oil paintings carry throughout the room in traditional Southern style.

ABOVE: An heirloom mahogany bureau takes center stage in the family room between the two windows. A Schumacher chintz, stacks familial oils and painted lamps create elegant columns against the knotted raffia grass cloth.

OPPOSITE: In a nod to Southern vernacular, we designed transoms to span the cased openings between the dining and into the music room beyond. I love to mix genres and furniture styles. An antique dining table is surrounded by freshly upholstered chairs. A Lewis and Wood scenic paper depicting deer and foliage wraps the dining room, while reclaimed brick pavers unify the two rooms.

PREVIOUS OVERLEAF: In the dining room, Lewis and Wood "Sitka," depicting deer and foliage, dances along the walls and is framed with a Schumacher damask on the windows. A custom chandelier with metal oak leaves echoes the flora just beyond. Exposed rafters and painted planks on the ceiling are tied to the horizontal paneling in color and texture. Blue and white accents are found in the lamps here and throughout the house.

OPPOSITE AND ABOVE: The music room is swathed in a striped grass cloth by Hartmann & Forbes above the horizontal paneling, creating a perpendicular cadence. The family's heirloom baby grand is the pivotal piece, dividing the space between music room and dining room, like a watershed. A sisal rug in the music area further delineates the space from the dining area at the other end.

LEFT AND OVERLEAF: The family room, or keeping room, off the kitchen is a playful but still elegant appointment of furniture, textures and styles. From reupholstered wing chairs to an antelope-pattern carpet, this room is to be enjoyed by the family comfortably and cozily. A velvet sofa depicting field and forest animals is whimsical but durable for this growing group of grandchildren. Heart pine built-ins display familial photos, books and other accumulated treasures.

Green cabinets and open shelves nod to classic kitchens but are in sync with today's color aesthetic. A Brunschwig and Fils pattern in soft greens and blues serves as the window treatment, while a sturdy outdoor fabric is used on the barstools.

ABOVE: The cypress and heart pine bar serves as the hyphen connecting the study and keeping room. Brass-and-glass shelving lightens the heavier wood tones and serves for display and storage too.

OPPOSITE: In the study, an Oushak rug sets a groundwork for accents of red and blue. Scalamandré tiger-print pillows and a collection of antique bird prints further enhance this gentleman's room.

THE MOUNTAINS ARE CALLING

When a couple of dear friends called me about a project in Cashiers, North Carolina, I was surprised when they told me where the project was exactly—it was in my neighborhood! Thrilled to have friends as neighbors too, I could not think of a better addition to our community than these folks. Downsizing from a larger home and sizable piece of mountain property, this cottage gave them all the right elements to embark on a fun new project.

It is often the case with homes in Cashiers that they have been summer retreats, used for a season and then the occupants return to their primary homes for the majority of the year. However, as people begin to spend longer than just a season in this magnificent locale, they realize it's time to update their homes. Creature comforts, more appropriate appointments and furnishings and the reflection of living here through several seasons has changed—for the better—this sleepy hamlet outside of Highlands, North Carolina.

Plaids, floral and warm patinas meld together against linen white painted paneling. Chandelier is by Paul Ferrante.

There are four distinct seasons in Cashiers, and each one has wondrous natural phenomena, such as cool evenings in the summer amongst lush ferns and foliage, spectacularly brilliant fall colors, cheery holiday lights and Christmas tree farms and amazing wintertime views, and then the renewal of it all with spring on the mountains in bright greens verdantly heralding the new season. With so much natural beauty and seasonal offerings, my team wanted to provide these clients with a cottage inspired by the colors and hues of the mountains and their flora.

Fresh, creamy white paneling updated the darker stained boards and set a crisper backdrop for vibrant patterns and colors. A new set of built-ins anchors one wall of the great room and balances the stone fireplace. Brown quickly becomes overworked in this neck of the woods—from the floors to the walls to the ceilings and furniture. I love each of those elements, but not all together. I told my clients, "No teddy bears, no bad plaid," as had become the kitschy combo in many mountain homes.

A bolder, leafy buffalo check plaid sofa pairs with an English Colefax and Fowler wool plaid on armchairs rectifies the "bad plaid" mantra as chic versions of tired patterns, while Carleton V chintzes printed on linen as opposed to polished cotton allows a more relaxed feel for the window treatments and upholstery too. Layers such as jute rugs atop white oak floors stained in a warm coffee hue are topped with vibrant tribal rugs. Pecky cypress is a classic backdrop for the shelving and is a handsome carved wet bar.

Divided into a dining and living room, this space needed another statement on the wall opposite the fireplace, but not necessarily another significant architectural statement. Enter one of my favorite tricks of the trade—a dazzling display of dishes! Blame it on my English heritage, but I am always a fan of plates and platters adorning the wall in a wonderful array. Here, cresting above and around a French *vaisselier* is a part of the client's amazing collection of transferware and English china. I often tell my clients that plates, unless filled with delicious food, are no good hiding in a cupboard! I am so thankful for friends such as these—especially when I'm asked to dine with them, for the wife is an excellent cook.

The kitchen needed to be efficient and personable, dotted with the right amount of pizazz. Apple green cabinets, butcher block counters and open shelving displaying further collections of amazing dinnerware, serving pieces and cookbooks from around the world give personality to this updated galley-style kitchen.

One of my favorite color combinations is a twist on a traditional scheme—complementary colors but dialed into their jewel and precious stone tones. Red and green become ruby and citrine, while orange and blue glow as topaz, garnet, andesine, lapis, sapphire and turquoise. For the bedroom at this mountain cottage, an antique Persian rug with all these colors inspired the room's palette.

This mountain cottage lives large—with great food, beautiful flowers and a family that fills it with laughter. Selfishly, when I can walk over for dinner or have cocktails on the porch, it makes the project that much more delightful.

The wood patina of an antique French vaisselier stands out on the painted board-and-batten walls. French porcelain figurines are now lamps that shed light onto this wonderful display.

ABOVE: A faux bamboo bar is carved and turned from cypress. Since the majority of the woodwork is painted, the natural finish of the cypress is a nice contrast and warm balance.

RIGHT: A Carleton V chintz printed on linen hangs at the windows and covers the armchairs as well. Lamps on mismatched end tables are by Georgia potter Charlie West, glazed in a wonderful shade of Carolina blue. On the back wall are whimsical sconces from designer Bunny Williams's line for Currey & Company.

OVERLEAF: A vivacious piece by artist Kay Flierl is a pop of color and a contemporary component against the ruggedness of the stacked stone. Pottery by Vicky Miller in a honey-toned mustard glaze adorns the mantel, and pieces are artfully displayed in the shelves too. A wool plaid on side chairs pulls color from the chintz, and a Cowtan & Tout tiger print woven is worn by an ottoman.

LEFT AND ABOVE: The mountains' kaleidoscope of greens were the inspiration for the verdant kitchen cabinets and ceiling. Whether in the darkest of winter or fullness of summer, greens are evident in this locale. Open shelves allow for display and easy access to cookbooks and serving pieces. A tribal runner in vivid jewel tones contrasts against the darker stained oak floors. Butcher block countertops and an apron-front sink keep the casual feel for this kitchen, while a cafe curtain at the box bay adds another pop of texture and color.

ABOVE: Turquoise accents emphasize pull from the rug color and set off the antique dresser, while vintage Italian wheat sheat sconces flank the mirror.

OPPOSITE: The citrine damask wallpaper, the pillow and window shade fabric, piping and monograms on the linens as well as accents in the artwork run the gamut of jewel-toned greens. Accents of lapis and turquoise are seen in the antique gin and rum jar lamps. A Jane Shelton floral in a golden hue is box pleated as a bed skirt and on the vintage bamboo settee.

I'LL BE HOME FOR CHRISTMAS

When the opportunity for a place of my own in the Cashiers presented itself, I was thrilled! Cashiers, North Carolina, has been a happy place for my family for generations. Farmdale will always be my home, but this home away from home has proved to be an exciting new chapter in my life. From hosting friends for Thanksgiving or enjoying the seasons and a different climate, I find the pace and place to be a good balance to home and work.

My favorite wildflower native to the area is the Joe Pye weed. It bolts up during the summer and is crested by lavender-periwinkle panicle blossoms that bring to mind that glorious time between summer and fall—a season when peaches meet apples, ferns meet golden foliage and the Joe Pye weed towers over hydrangeas. When a cottage needing some renovation came my way, "Joe Pye Cottage" simply felt like an apropos name.

I adore red and "carl" together at the holidays, and my friend Libby Endry helped make my first holiday season at Joe Pye magical with red peonies, perfectly peachy Free Spirit roses, amaryllis, magnolia and nandina boughs.

High Hampton has for centuries been a haven and retreat from the heat for Southerners, and with the summertime sweltering, many families escape the heat in the cooler altitude. My new retreat home in those mountains was structurally in good shape, so I focused on the aesthetics and floor plan. Taking a former deck and sunroom into the fold, I was able to create a dining room proper, and thus the valuable real estate of the main room did not have to be shared by living and dining arrangements. One of my favorite room arrangements is a main sofa, two chairs flanking it and two smaller sofas as well at the fireplace. This allows gracious sitting room for a crowd and conversation but still is cozy enough if it's just me catching up on *The Crown* on a Sunday night.

All frames and fabrics of the living room pieces are by Thibaut. The entire color scheme for the home comes from the coromandel screen that commands the main wall in my living room. My friend and talented designer Jett Thompson found it and bought it on the spot for me—knowing I was good for it. She called and said, "I found a forever piece for you—a screen—and it's 'carl'" (my mother referred to the color "coral" as "carl," and I inherited her love for the color). When I saw the screen, it was love at first sight. Carl, olive green, honey gold, tawny taupe, soft French gray-blue and verdant hues were all pulled from the screen's colorway and carried throughout the home—inside and out.

The new dining room is voluminous but not large in square footage. So, the challenge presented was solved with serving pieces at either end instead of the sides of the table. A madras-meets-ikat plaid in an aqua tone by Brunschwig and Fils covers the new chairs set around an old pine drop-leaf table.

The bedrooms were assigned according to my expected guests—two in particular: my nephew, Napp, and niece, Sally James. Each room sports two beds, so I can host them and their family and friends easily.

As for my room, I wanted a soothing palette of soft greens, lichen, cream and warm colors for the furniture pieces. "Squirrel and Sunflower" by Mark Hearld lines the walls, and various wood finishes on the furniture add further warmth.

Porches in Cashiers boast top billing in the summer and fall, and I wanted to fully embrace mine in the mountains. Outdoor fabrics drape and frame the porch and are carried onto the furniture too. Breezes are easily captured here, and the chance to sit outdoors for a generous part of the year carries a nuance we Deep South dwellers don't often find.

Joe Pye Cottage is a refuge and respite. I love to entertain and recharge here. I love having the house filled with friends and family, and relish staying on my own and reading, building fires, writing or gardening with plants I cannot grow at Farmdale. It is a blessing beyond measure to call this place home as well.

OPPOSITE: I already owned a couple smaller pieces of Asheville artist Bee Sieburg's work when I ran into her at my friend Libby Endry's store, Gardener's Cottage. Bee was telling me about a painting of sheep she had recently finished. The next thing I knew, I had commissioned Bee to paint a mountain landscape with sheep—complete with Joe Pye Weed in their field. The painting is perfect atop my mantel, flanked with green-glazed Mediterranean pottery vessels that I fill with seasonal clippings.

OVERLEAF: Thibaut "Papagayo" in a green tea hue adorns the boxy wing chairs in the living room and frames the windows and doors leading to the porch. A mix of Charlie West pottery lamps and tea caddy lamps light the space.

ABOVE: Beneath the staircase, a French cherry buffet with scrolled feet and a carved sunflower serves as additional storage and sports a prized brass deer I found at an antique shop along the way.

RIGHT: Two seating groups make for conversation, relaxing or taking in television or the view. The facing sofas are perfect for fireside reading or a long winter's nap. The Chatham-style sofa is covered in a mossy green channel-quilted velvet, a handsome comple-ment to the floral-covered wing chairs in "Papagayo" by Thibaut. I carried the porch blue ceiling inside, as the room's large plate glass window connects the two spaces.

OPPOSITE: An oval table displays part of my collection of cream-ware tureens. Charlie West pottery holds seasonal branches. An Asian bench allows for extra seating at the table or elsewhere in the room. Thibaut "Papagayo" frames the window looking onto the porch.

ABOVE: A French walnut buffet boasts handsome brass hinges and escutcheons with a floral and vine carving. This is one of the favorite pieces I own. Atop are a pair of Charlie West lamps in a custom glaze that changes with the light—ranging from deep, lagoon blue to teal to blue, depending on the light. A gilded Louis Philippe mirror with beading and a crested arch is flanked with French majolica asparagus plates. Season's offerings sit atop the buffet—such as persimmons, stick candles and roses.

ABOVE: A favorite taxidermy pheasant looks dashingly handsome "in flight" as a holiday centerpiece.

RIGHT: An Italian demilune anchors one end, and with its whitewashed patina, iron stretchers and elegant curve, it is truly a good server and display piece for the room. I carried the Thibaut "Papagayo" in here on the windows, as this room opens right into the living room.

LEFT: A madras-meets-ikat plaid in an aqua tone by Brunschwig and Fils covers the new chairs set around an old pine drop-leaf table. Seagrass, jute and sisal rugs throughout the home enable the layering of smaller rugs for texture and color or to neutrally unify a room.

ABOVE: On the largest wall of the room, I did not have the depth for a piece of furniture; however, the wall height provided an opportunity. Framing panels of a Phillip Jeffries scenic grass cloth as a tryptic gave the presence and visual weight the wall needed. The white sisal woven grass cloth panels are a great complement to the chunkier raffia grass cloth of the walls. I rely on grass cloth to provide not only color but texture—an effect that paint alone cannot often achieve.

ABOVE: The repeat of Mark Hearld "Squirrel and Sunflower" pattern in a sage colorway gives life to the walls. My friend Erika Powell designed the fabric for the windows and the Euros on the bed too, which painted Benjamin Moore "Mopboard Black" is just dark enough to be striking but not overly bold.

OPPOSITE: An antique English mahogany breakfront secretary, French faux bamboo chests and an Irish pine table add patina and warmth as well as function to the room.

ABOVE: A large-scale piece of artwork from Massey Gordon in Perry is the focal on one wall; its colors spoke to me for Sally James's room, and she adores animals.

RIGHT: In Sally James's room, I decided to fully embrace "carl" with peach, pink and shell and shades therein. White rattan beds, tole floral lamps and Erika M. Powell Textiles "Kumquats" all meld together in a happy little girl's room. My mother's needlepoint rug adds pizzazz and nostalgia to the space.

OPPOSITE AND ABOVE: Napp's room is papered in a Thibaut trellis, and the bedding and windows sport a classic Scalamandré pattern, "Edwin's Covey." Handsome Stroheim checks coordinate in rooms throughout the house.

RIGHT: A bird dog by Georgia artist Derek Taylor is fitting with the "Edwin's Covey" fabric in the room. An English bowfront chest, French prayer chairs and alabaster lamps create an homage to some of my favorite things.

OPPOSITE: I call this guest room "Fern Suite," for the Thibaut fern fabric on the shams and window treatments and also for the view out the window to the beds of ferns that surround the home in summertime.

ABOVE LEFT: A tortoise-shell-finished rattan and bamboo headboard is a striking contrast with the wallpaper—a trellis motif created by tiny oak leaves.

ABOVE RIGHT: A tribal rug atop a soft jute gives some color to the ground plane of this room, while a midcentury Italian mirror, reminiscent of my crest with the garden tools and foliage, reflects the room.

LEFT: A porch is one of the things that makes a home in Cashiers such a treasure. Mine is furnished like another room of the house. A vintage sign I found at Scott's Antique Market years ago now has its home on the porch. The aquas, blues and reds are fun with the caramel and cinnamon plaid and ticking. Seasonal plantings and arrangements that change throughout the year make the porch a frequent destination to enjoy the environment.

ABOVE: Fresh updates of plaids, ferns and other foliage prints abound in my mountain home. Lamp shades of a Scalamandré fern print top confit-jar lamps from Vivienne Metzger Antiques in the perfect shade of mustard.

A TIME
TO WED

For my sister Meredith and her fiancé, Keaton (now husband), a wedding at home on our family's land was simply the only plan. Our sister, Maggie, and her husband, Zach, had their reception on the land, as did our cousin Kasi and her husband, Brennan, following a tradition of so many Southern families who host family functions on the land where their family has lived, farmed or worked. Most of the time, our barn houses the tractor and a ski boat, but the place becomes a lovely pavilion dressed in lights!

Elegance and classic décor were Meredith's wishes. "Beautiful and Southern," "appropriate and hospitable," and "genuine and enjoyable" all became words to focus on for the big day. Meredith and Keaton's ceremony

I hosted the ceremony at Farmdale, where guests were greeted with champagne and crab cakes from The Perfect Pear. La Tavola Linens skirt the tables. Florals by Luella Floral were sumptuously arranged in shades of soft creams, pinks, greenery from the land and antique hydrangeas.

OPPOSITE: Upon entering Farmdale, the dining is just inside the double doors. Antique bricks were used for the flooring, as my dining room also doubles as a reception hall or foyer. A welcome arrangement of roses, lilies, delphinium and hydrangea billows from an antique urn.

ABOVE LEFT: A favored familial piece, an English Ironstone platter holds center stage on my antique chinoiserie sideboard. Italian birds from Bruner Antiques, silver candlesticks, a majolica platter and a majolica compote round out this collection of heirlooms and treasured objects. The four flanking original watercolors by Darby Boruff showcase my favorite specimens of Georgia floral and fauna.

ABOVE RIGHT: The chinoiserie panel is a framed fragment of a hand-painted wallpaper.

ABOVE AND OPPOSITE: The painted horizontal and vertical paneling in my stairwell allows architectural elements, antiques and heirlooms to shine. The Chippendale railing is an homage to noted architect Frank McCall's home at Sea Island. Pops of color are seen in the majolica plates, tobacco leaf lamp and Italian blue ducks. Antique oils, framed ornithology prints and a needlepoint bell pull all serve as artwork in this space. The mahogany block chest with handsome brass escutcheons is topped with flowers to celebrate the day. I love to keep fresh flowers here, but these peach roses, stock, lilies and hydrangeas will always remind me of Meredith's wedding.

OPPOSITE: My mother's amaryllis fireplace screen is a treasured heirloom. She always kept dried hydrangeas on her mantel, so I do as well. These are dried limelights from our home in Cashiers. My mantel is formal in style but relaxed as it is carved out of pecky cypress. A tribal runner is layered atop a jute rug, Taylor Burke Home sofas and plush pillows create a curated place to gather. Barn doors lead to a guest suite on the right and a built-in bar on the left. My Mimi's pagoda light fixture hangs above the space.

ABOVE: The view from the kitchen across the living is to the stairwell and back hall. Light from the garden shines through into this part of the home, which is outfitted with an antique bamboo étagère for displaying pottery and artwork. Spanish cedar beams and newel posts, heart pine floor and painted horizontal paneling meld with tufted furniture, grass cloth and collected artwork in my living room.

OPPOSITE: For my front portico, Robert Norris designed a double staircase to frame a welcoming bed for my syrup kettle and millstone fountain. I love symmetry to set the scene, and then "gild the lily" with organic forms, such as perennial and seasonal plantings. The wreaths and garland add a festive nod to the special day.

ABOVE: Since my house is set within the woods, I chose a deep, dark chocolate brown for the home and rosemary green shutters. This allows greens and white to pop and the house to meld with the setting.

was held at my home, Farmdale, in the garden proper, as family and friends gathered for an intimate ceremony officiated by our cousin-in-law Brennan.

For such an event, I called in the dream team to execute Meredith's vision. Though handy as host, I wanted to enjoy the day as a participant and spectator and brother of bride, to tire from dancing, not hanging garlands. As our father walked Meredith down the aisle—the brick garden pathway connecting the home and garden—I shed a tear of pure joy! The planning and setting of this garden had come to fruition. My hope is that my home and garden will always be a refuge of peace, love and wonderful memories of this special day and more to come.

After the ceremony, the bridal party and guests made their way down to the pavilion at our aunt and uncle's house. Our aunt and uncle are our second set of parents more so and live on the land too. The buffet was a *fête accomplis* of Southern culinary delights and erupted with a larger-than-life centerpiece—complete with scuppernong vines from our woods, Ligustrum berries, roses, branches and boughs of willow and magnolia bursting forth from an antique iron font.

Meredith wanted her wedding cake to be the centerpiece of the pavilion—our family puts dessert as top billing! Lisa Mae Cakes made the divine tiered cake that rested atop an heirloom cake stand, while our beloved Mimi and Granddaddy's cake topper made a cameo appearance.

Father of the Bride and *Steel Magnolias* are two of Meredith's favorite movies. Both depict families preparing for a wedding at home along with all the idiosyncrasies, local personalities and family dynamics that bubble to the surface with an event like this. One trademark scene in *Steel Magnolias* portrays Southerners in a hilarious light—revealing our quirky side and translating that into food. Loosely quoted from the movie: "Jackson wanted a cake in the shape of an armadillo. He has an aunt that makes them . . . The cake part is red velvet cake. Blood red!" Keaton's favorite cake is red velvet, so an armadillo groom's cake was apropos!

The flowers at the ceremony and reception were all in honor of the love of Meredith's and Keaton's grandparents—and our mama, whose spirit was undoubtedly there. The wedding day will always be a remarkable, truly memorable event for our family.

The axis from my front door to my back door runs all the way to this focal point, where the small patio is just the right size for garden furniture and entertaining. The bricks are a blend of antebellum style from Cherokee Brick in Macon. The silhouette of the shallow arch and flared sides is roughly mimicked in the font basin's wall. Papyrus shoots from the water basin while antique fruit basket finials flank the wall on the columns.

ABOVE: I plant all green and white foliage and flowers in my garden. Pops of color bloom seasonally, but I try to keep it classically green and white. This color combo is visually cooling and apropos throughout the year. The faux bois benches are by Currey and Company.

OPPOSITE: A former well font is now a planter in my garden, filled with mums, lamb's ear and mandavilla. Boxwood hedges are interplanted with 'Little Lamb' hydrangeas and the garden gate is seen just beyond, flanked by antique pineapple finials atop the brick pillars.

LEFT: An antique church steeple is the center point of my garden. I love to the rusty patina of the Gothic architecture. White mums, sedum and euphorbia bloom around the steeple for autumnal touches.

ABOVE: For the planters around Farmdale, I planted mixes of my favorite fall flowers and foliage too. Mexican salvia, lamb's ear and angel vine billow out of mossy terra-cotta pots.

OPPOSITE: My friend Henry Hines found millstones that had split. I used them as threshold markers entering the garden. The garden gates were adorned with floral wreaths of soft peach roses, eucalyptus and hydrangea.

The main brick pathway served as the "aisle" for the ceremony. My garden wall fountain was the backdrop for the ceremony, which was reflected by an antique French zinc architectural element turned into a mirror. My nephew, Napp, expresses his sentiment as any six-year-old does when the officiator says "You may kiss the bride."

OPPOSITE: The buffet was a spread the likes of which I had hardly seen before! Apple cobbler with ice cream made on the spot was a nod to the season. Honey Catering knocked it out of the park!

ABOVE LEFT AND RIGHT The divine tiered cake that rested atop an heirloom cake stand was made by Lisa Mae Cakes, while our beloved Mimi and Granddaddy's cake topper made a cameo appearance.

LEFT: As in the movie *Steel Magnolias*, we had Lisa Mae make the groom's cake in the shape of an armadillo. It is our ability to meld the odd and the ordinary that makes our Southern culture extraordinary.

The flowers at the ceremony and reception were all in honor of the love of the bride and groom's grandparents—and our Mama, whose spirit was undoubtedly there. The wedding day will always be a truly memorable event for our family.

ACKNOWLEDGMENTS

When it comes to acknowledging those who are a part of my village, tribe, team and family, the words "thank you" seem to fall short—but these two little words are sincerely expressed. To my staff and team players at James Farmer Inc.: you ladies make the dream possible. Margaret, Melanie, Jesse, Haley, Caroline, Ashley—thank you! Lizzie and Corie, welcome to the team! Exciting opportunities on the horizon for us all. And to my friends Kayla and George Bruner for helping me move into Joe Pye and for simply being my friends every day. The wedding was wonderful!

Our design visions for our clients are made possible by their trust in us. That trust and working relationship is a "good and perfect gift." Thank you for opening your homes and allowing the James Farmer Inc. team to turn your houses into homes. Many thanks to Brandy and Mitchell Martin, Beth and Mike Phelps, Catherine and Evrard Fraise, Donna and Mark Miller, Brenda and Chop Evans, Ashley and Matt Forrest, and Karen and Fred Hirons for all you do for us and so many others. Your homes are indelibly placed in my heart.

To Rhett Bonner and the team of Bonner Buchanan Homes, it was a pleasure to work on two custom homes you built.

To my architect and friend Robert Norris and his amazing team, thank you for designing the place I call home; I look forward to arriving home every single day.

To my family and friends who love and support me and encourage me to dream and design and, thank you and love you!

These wonderful images are captured by the talented, skilled photography of Jeff Herr. Thank you, Jeff, for your cooperation and participation. My longtime friend and photography Emily Followill contributed the Oak Bowery images—thank you, my dear! Amber Joy, friend of the Farmer children for years, you and Tyler captured Meredith's special day romantically perfect! Thank you, Joy and Everette Photography! Thank you Nancy Kuperberg and the No Regrets planning team for all your hard work and dedication. Thank you, Luella Floral, Honey Catering and Rental Concepts for all you did!

Our seamstresses, architects, workrooms, installers, antique dealers, vendors and design reps—y'all are true treasures in our industry. Thank you for all you do for my company.

Thank you, Madge Baird, my editor extraordinaire at Gibbs Smith. You have believed in me since day one. That will always be the highest honor! Thank you to Rita Sowins for your fine book design.

To my fellow "Perrysian" and dear friend Deborah Roberts, thank you for writing the foreword to this book. You truly understand the feeling of "arriving home" and have set a wonderful example of taste, talent and warmth for your family and friends. I am so proud of all you have accomplished in your career; yet, I am prouder still to call you my friend.

My friend and fellow gardener Mary Royal, thank you for growing gorgeous flowers and herbs seen throughout the pages of this book. You brighten the lives of so many with your dahlias, roses, zinnias and wonderful personality.

My niece, Sally James, epitomizes the exuberance everyone felt on this special wedding day.

First Edition
20 21 22 23 24   5 4 3 2 1

Published by
Gibbs Smith
P.O. Box 667
Layton, Utah 84041
1.800.835.4993 orders
www.gibbs-smith.com

Designed by Rita Sowins / Sowins Design
Printed and bound in Hong Kong, China

Gibbs Smith books are printed on paper produced from sustainable PEFC-certified forest/controlled wood source.
Learn more at www.pefc.org.
Printed and bound in Hong Kong

Library of Congress Cataloging-in-Publication Data

Names: Farmer, James T., III, author. | Herr, Jeff, 1963- photographer.
Title: Arriving home : a gracious Southern welcome / James T. Farmer ;
Deborah Roberts (foreword) ; photographs by Jeff Herr.
Description: First edition. | Layton, Utah : Gibbs Smith, [2020] | Summary:
"Traditional style stands the test of time. That is the mantra for James   Farmer's aesthetic. Classic tastes melded
with fresh approaches for how we live and love in homes. In these homes across the Atlantic side of
the country, high style and relaxed comfort are displayed hand in hand. Discover antiques mixed with new upholstery,
collections and art displayed against pattern and textured wall coverings, and layers of
jute, sisal, and wood grounding the floors while doses of intentional color keep the rooms personable. From a grand
Connecticut country home to a stately St. Louis house or a columned antebellum Alabama home,
Farmer's style travels the country to set the tone for the lives of his clients. Homes in the city, the mountains, the
country, and coastal locales all reflect in this journey while being rooted in Southern design."-- Provided by publisher.
Identifiers: LCCN 2020000161 | ISBN 9781423654131 (hardcover) | ISBN
9781423653158 (epub)
Subjects: LCSH: Interior decoration--Southern States. | Architecture,
Domestic--Southern States.
Classification: LCC NK2006 .F37 2020 | DDC 747.0975--dc23
LC record available at https://lccn.loc.gov/2020000161